T0195965

A Glimpse into Time

Time

A.R. SMITH

Archway Publishing books may be ordered through booksellers or by contacting:

Archway Publishing
1663 Liberty Drive
Bloomington, IN 47403
www.archwaypublishing.com
844-669-3957

ISBN: 978-1-4808-9416-7 (sc)
ISBN: 978-1-4808-9417-4 (e)

Print information available on the last page.

Archway Publishing rev. date: 03/30/2021

A Glimpse into Time

This book belongs to

_____

Elizabeth Bessie Coleman

Born in Texas, she was the first black woman or man to have a pilot license.

Studying in France and having attended Langston University, Bessie Coleman was one of the best aviators of her time.

Lewis Howard Latimer

Was a draftsman for the patents of the lightbulb and telephone. Latimer was a genius and a trend setter before his time. Born in Chelsea Massachusetts, Latimer also created a system to improve toilets for railroad carts.

Fig 1

Fig 2

Fig 3

Rebecca lee Crumpler

A lady for the children, Mrs. Crumpler was the first African American woman doctor of medicine. She performed her job mostly on poor women and children. Born in Delaware, Mrs. Crumpler had a goodwill and the biggest heart.

Grandville Tailer Woods

Born in Ohio, Grandville was a chief engineer who focused mainly on trains and street cars. He is also credited for inventing the air brake for trains.

Grandville was a supreme mechanic and a smart man.

Sarah Boone

Born as Sarah Marshall she invented improvements for the ironing board. Her upgrades to the ironing board helped the quality of ironing. Coming from North Carolina, Sarah Boone understood the importance of appearance.

Paul R. Williams

Born in Los Angeles with a unique talent for building, Paul Williams was an outstanding architect. Credited with designing YMCA buildings, churches, and a host of housing developments, Mr. Williams is responsible for designing over 2,000 buildings.

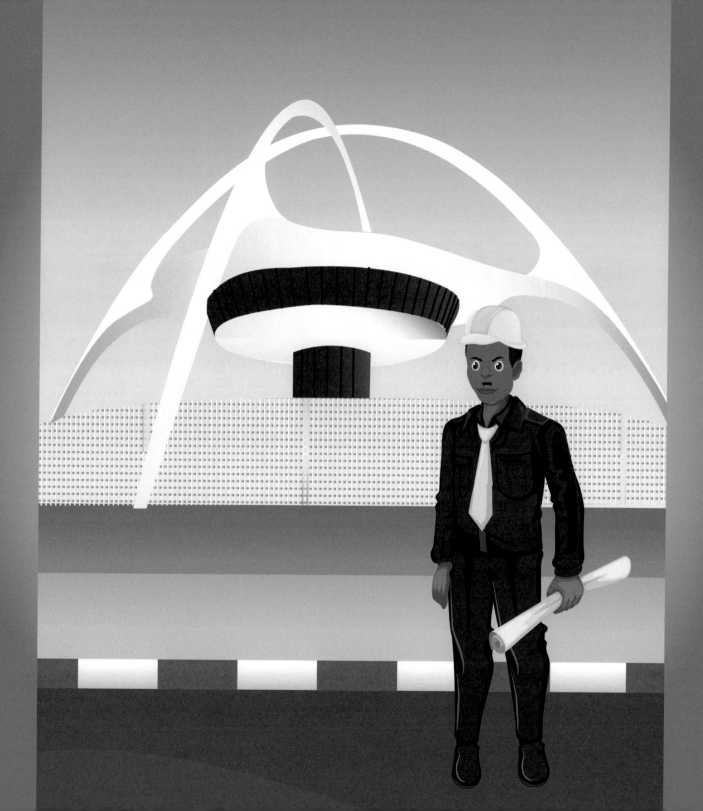

Marie Van Brittan Brown

Ahead of her time, Marie Brown was a forward thinker. Coming from Jamaica Queens, New York she invented the home security system.

With television monitoring and wireless radio control this invention helped make homes safer.

James Derham

By 15 Mr. Derham was well versed in studying medicine. Also having the ability to speak French, Spanish, and English James was an intelligent man. Specializing in throat diseases James Derham was an extraordinary doctor.

Biddy Mason

Born in Hancock County Georgia, Mason moved to California. She was one of the first African Americans to own land. A woman of many skills such as nursing and medicines. Biddy would go on to own a lot of land and become one of the wealthiest women in the country.

Horace King

When talking about architects Horace is one of the elites. Born in South Carolina and well respected for bridge building, Mr. King constructed many churches, homes, and bridges in the south. Very good with his hands and mind Horace King is known as the King and Prince of bridge builders.

Phillis Wheatley

Was the first African American author to write poetry. Born in West Africa and raised in Boston, by age 12 Phillis was already advanced in reading Greek and Latin. Ms. Wheatley had a great literary ability and published many poems.

Benjamin Banneker

Was a surveyor and also creator of the almanac.

Born in Baltimore, Maryland Benjamin had supreme mathematics and knowledge of the stars. He was the main surveyor of Washington D.C .

About the Author

Amen Smith was born and raised in Boston, Massachusetts. Coming from a humble and educated household, he graduated from college with a degree in arts and science. As a person that believes in ownership and being entrepreneurial, he published this book to enlighten readers.

Printed in the United States
by Baker & Taylor Publisher Services